HOW MAJESTIC IS *Thy Name*

NEW LEAF PRESS
www.newleafpress.net

HOW MAJESTIC IS Thy Name

Copyright© 2001 New Leaf Press / Master Books, Green Forest, Arkansas

Concept, design and production by Left Coast Design, Portland, Oregon.

ISBN: 0-89221-507-0   Library of Congress: 2001-090996   Printed in the United States of America.

All Photography by **Steve Terrill**, Portland, Oregon, unless otherwise indicated.

Digital Stock, pages 4, 5, 36-39, 41, 56, 57

Gene Moore, pages 46, 47

FPG, pages 62. 63

Image Bank, pages 26 (right), 30 (right), 34, 42 43, 48-55 (left), 60, 61, 69 (large)

Masterfile, page 44

National Geographic, pages 28, 29, 55 (right)

Photo Disc, pages 6-13, 15-17, 26 (left)

Superstock, pages 58, 59

Tony Stone, page 70

Please visit our website for other great titles: WWW.NEWLEAFPRESS.NET

For information regarding publicity contact New Leaf Press at 870-438-5288

O LORD,
OUR LORD,
HOW MAJESTIC
IS YOUR NAME
IN ALL THE
EARTH! *Psalm 8:1*

TABLE OF CONTENTS

F rom the very beginning, human beings have craned their necks toward the night sky and stared in wonder at the stars. How many there are! How tiny! And so near, it seems as though one could reach out and touch them   ◆   This is one case where appearances can badly mask the truth. For in reality, the universe contains untold trillions of stars, not the mere thousands that can be seen from earth by the naked eye. Some 100 billion stars light up the Milky Way galaxy alone — and the cosmos harbors billions of galaxies, some vastly larger than our own ◆ And tiny? Hardly. Some of those twinkling little specks of light — such as the red giant Betelgeuse — are actually up to 500 times larger than our own sun. Of course, other stars may take up far less space. A star massive enough to create a supernova, for example, may after the explosion shrink to a sphere no larger than twelve to thirty miles in diameter. But don't plan on visiting it any time soon; it would still have a mass several times that of the sun and a density millions of times greater. A teaspoon of it would weigh thousands of tons   ◆   And forget about near. The closest star to earth is Proxima Centauri. If you could travel at the speed of light, it would take you 4.3 years to get there — but at the fastest speeds humankind has thus far achieved, it would take almost 280 centuries. When you consider that the Milky Way galaxy alone stretches some 70,000 light years across, you stop talking about "near."

AND YET...

God not only created the stars (Genesis 1:16), He set each one in place (Psalm 8:3). The stars may look impossibly bright to us, but in His eyes not even the stars are pure (Job 25:5). The Psalmist calls upon the stars to praise God (Psalm 148:3) and our Lord warns us not to worship the starry host (Deuteronomy 4:19). Though they stagger us, they hide no secrets from Him:

HE DETERMINES THE NUMBER OF THE STARS AND CALLS THEM EACH BY NAME. GREAT IS OUR LORD AND MIGHTY IN POWER; HIS UNDERSTANDING HAS NO LIMIT.

(PSALM 147:4-5)

I t may look like a tiny eyeball peering through the sky's backyard fence, but our sun has a volume 1.3 million times that of the earth and accounts for 99.8 percent of the total mass of the solar system. It looks so small because we're in orbit at a distance of nearly 93 million miles. Good thing we're that far away, too. If you dared to touch it, you'd instantly vaporize from its surface temperature of about 10,000 degrees Fahrenheit — chilly by comparison to the solar core, which burns at an impossible 27 million degrees. The sun continually turns hydrogen into

SUN

helium through the process of fusion, converting 4 million tons of matter into energy every second ✦ Astronomers consider the sun to be an average star in mass, size, and brightness, and say that if it continued on an average course, it would eventually become a red giant, engulf Mercury and Venus, blow away the earth's atmosphere and boil its oceans. In the end it would turn into a white dwarf star — a solid ball about the size of earth, with a density 50,000 times that of water, perhaps covered by a thin layer of ice and an atmosphere a few yards thick. But don't be too alarmed; scientists figure such a catastrophe won't happen for a very, *very* long time ✦ Light from the sun makes possible all life on earth. When we burn wood or coal, we're actually releasing stored

energy from the sun. And more than light reaches us from our star. Solar winds — charged particles continually flowing from the sun's corona — move through space at speeds of more than 400 miles per second, reaching at least to the orbit of Neptune. When gigantic magnetic storms on the sun (some measuring 31,000 miles across) eject strong solar winds toward earth, they produce spectacular "Northern Lights" displays on some parts of our planet through interaction with earth's atmosphere. Nothing mankind has conceived can rival the sun.

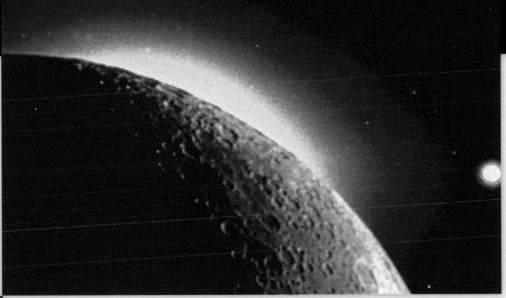

K nowing that humans would be tempted to worship the sun He created, God called it merely a "greater light to govern the day" (Genesis 1:16). The sun may be mighty, but when the Lord orders it to retreat, it hustles backwards (Isaiah 38:8). Even if He should command it to stop shining, it would instantly go black (Job 9:7). God uses the power of the sun to strengthen us, so that from the rising of the sun to the place of its setting men may know there is none besides Him.

I AM THE LORD, AND THERE IS NO OTHER.

I FORM THE LIGHT AND CREATE DARKNESS,

I BRING PROSPERITY AND CREATE DISASTER;

I, THE LORD, DO ALL THESE THINGS.

(ISAIAH 45:6-7)

EARTH

Speeding around the sun at 18.5 miles per second, the earth completes one orbit every 365 days, rotating on its axis every 23 hours, 56 minutes and 4 seconds. Its slightly elliptical orbit of almost 93 million miles from the sun provides exactly the right conditions for life to flourish. Any closer to its star, and the planet's water would vaporize; any further away, and it would freeze solid ◆ Living creatures on earth breathe an atmosphere composed of about 78 percent nitrogen, 21 percent oxygen, with the rest comprised of argon, water vapor, carbon dioxide, and other gases. This mixture prevents most ultraviolet light from reaching the planet's surface; without such a screen, life as we know it could not exist ◆ The earth boasts a mass of approximately 6×10^{21} metric tons and a surface area of about 197 million square miles. A crust about 21 miles thick lies under the continents; it shrinks to three miles under the oceans. Beneath the crust stretches a mantle about 1,800

miles deep; below that lies a molten core composed mostly of iron. This core likely is divided into two parts, an outer, fluid region, and an extremely dense, solid region about 1,500 miles across — all extremely hot. It is estimated that an electric current constantly flowing in the outer core generates approximately 90 percent of earth's magnetic field. This magnetosphere extends about 90 miles above the earth's surface, trapping rapidly moving charged particles emanating from solar winds. Without this magnetic shield, all life on earth would perish in a bombardment of deadly cosmic radioactivity. What a complex, unique marvel is the earth!

AND YET...

Although top scientists are only beginning to understand the sophisticated design of our planet, without the slightest effort God has always fully "comprehended the vast expanses of the earth" (Job 38:18). It is He who "suspends the earth over nothing" (Job 26:7) and He who "sits enthroned above the circle of the earth" (Isaiah 40:22). No wonder the Psalmist exclaims, "How awesome is the LORD Most High, the great King over all the earth!" (Psalm 47:2), for as Jeremiah says,

GOD MADE THE EARTH BY HIS POWER; HE FOUNDED THE WORLD BY HIS WISDOM.

(JEREMIAH 10:12)

The moon boasts a diameter of 2,160 miles, about a third that of the earth. While to us it seems to shine bright in the clear night sky, it actually reflects only about 7.3 percent of the sunlight that strikes it. It rotates on its axis every 29 days, identical to the time it takes to complete its orbit around earth — which explains why it always shows us the same face. Some of the craters pockmarking its surface measure more than 125 miles wide, with ridges rising almost a mile high   •   At the surface of the earth the gravitational force of the moon measures about 2.2 times greater than that of the sun. Every day the moon silently lifts the world's oceans—vast basins of water soundlessly and irresistibly heaved into the air. In Boston the tide recedes ten feet. In Eastport, Maine, it recedes nineteen feet. In Nova Scotia's Bay of Fundy, the tide varies up to forty-three feet. If the moon were only 50,000 miles away from earth instead of 240,000, gigantic tides would submerge all the continents under water; even the highest mountains would slip beneath the waves   •   How awesome is the moon! If you stood on its surface, unprotected from the sun's ferocious radiation, the fluids in your body would boil; but if you walked into the shadow of a large rock, you would quickly freeze solid.

☾ MOON

AND YET...

To God the moon is nothing but a "lesser light to govern the night" (Genesis 1:16). When He commanded it to stay still in the sky, it instantly obeyed (Joshua 10:13). What we consider bright He sees as dark (Job 25:5) — and one day He will replace the light of the moon with the brilliance of His own glory:

THE SUN WILL NO MORE BE YOUR LIGHT BY DAY, NOR WILL THE BRIGHTNESS OF THE MOON SHINE ON YOU, FOR THE LORD WILL BE YOUR EVERLASTING LIGHT, AND YOUR GOD WILL BE YOUR GLORY.

(ISAIAH 60:19)

Millions of them silently fly around above you, and you'd better hope that one doesn't fall on your head. Asteroids may be the stuff of science fiction, but they're terribly real — as a visit to Canyon Diablo west of Winslow, Arizona, will attest ✦ Meteor Crater measures about 4,000 feet in diameter, with an interior depth of 600 feet and a rim rising 200 feet above the sur-

ASTEROIDS

rounding plain. A fallen asteroid created the crater at least 5000 years ago. The resulting explosion scattered fragments of nickel-iron (ranging in size from pebbles to 1,400 pounds) over 100 square miles ✦ The largest known asteroid in the Solar System, Ceres, measures 584 miles across. Astronomers have identified more than 250 asteroids with diameters of at least 62 miles, and believe more than a million rocks with diameters greater than half a mile orbit between Jupiter and Mars. Photographic evidence suggests our Moon is pockmarked with some 3 trillion asteroid-caused craters greater than three feet in diameter ✦ So is earth in danger from these space visitors? Judge for yourself. In 1992, a three-mile-long asteroid named Toutatis passed less than nine lunar distances from earth—and astronomers believe that in 2004 it will whiz by within 930,000 miles (less than four lunar distances). And that's just one asteroid we know about. Many such flying rocks don't reflect much light, so we can't see them until they're almost on top of us ✦ Scientists believe that asteroids with diameters of at least .6 miles periodically collide with earth, each with an explosive yield greater than several hydrogen bombs. Each collision would leave a crater 8 miles across and would cause short-term climatic changes worldwide. That's a lot of power just from a falling rock!

AND YET...

God knows the exact number of asteroids in the universe (Psalm 147:4). In fact, He personally set them in their proper places (Psalm 8:3). It is He who seals off their light (Job 9:7) and calls them "wandering stars, for whom blackest darkness has been reserved forever" (Jude 1:13). God says that in the day of His wrath "men will faint from terror, apprehensive of what is coming on the world, for the heavenly bodies will be shaken" (Luke 21:26), and He paints a startling picture of a future celestial judgment:

THE STARS IN THE SKY FELL TO EARTH, AS LATE FIGS DROP FROM A FIG TREE WHEN SHAKEN BY A STRONG WIND. THE SKY RECEDED LIKE A SCROLL, ROLLING UP, AND EVERY MOUNTAIN AND ISLAND WAS REMOVED FROM ITS PLACE. . . . SOMETHING LIKE A HUGE MOUNTAIN, ALL ABLAZE, WAS THROWN INTO THE SEA . . . AND A GREAT STAR, BLAZING LIKE A TORCH, FELL FROM THE SKY ON A THIRD OF THE RIVERS AND ON THE SPRINGS OF WATER.

(REVELATION 6:13, 14; 8:8, 10)

15

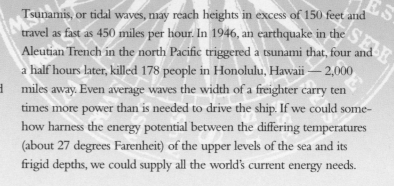

Oceans cover more than 70 percent of the earth's surface, to an average depth of 2.3 miles — a volume of water estimated at 329 million cubic miles (11 times the volume of dry land). The Mariana Trench, halfway between the Pacific islands of Guam and Yap, plunges to a depth of 36,200 feet, more than six and a half miles straight down. If the world's tallest mountain, Everest, were to be thrown into this watery hole, you'd still have to take a submarine down over 1.3 miles to reach the summit (and at those depths, the hull pressure on your submarine would amount to over 1,000 atmospheres) ◆ Of course, the ocean contains a lot more than water. If you were to remove all of its salt, you would harvest 50,000,000,000,000,000 tons of the stuff — enough to cover the entire planet in a layer 150 feet thick. Sea water also holds more gold than exists on land, 100 times as much as humans have mined throughout world history ◆ The size and power of the sea awes us, and rightly so.

Tsunamis, or tidal waves, may reach heights in excess of 150 feet and travel as fast as 450 miles per hour. In 1946, an earthquake in the Aleutian Trench in the north Pacific triggered a tsunami that, four and a half hours later, killed 178 people in Honolulu, Hawaii — 2,000 miles away. Even average waves the width of a freighter carry ten times more power than is needed to drive the ship. If we could somehow harness the energy potential between the differing temperatures (about 27 degrees Farenheit) of the upper levels of the sea and its frigid depths, we could supply all the world's current energy needs.

SEA

AND YET...

At a mere blast from the nostrils of God, the deep valleys of the sea lie exposed (Psalm 18:15). We may think the sea vast, but He can pour it all into little jars (Psalm 33:7). He quiets the raging sea with a single word (Psalm 89:9; Mark 4:39) and though the waves may roll and roar, they cannot cross the boundaries He has set for them (Job 38:10-11; Proverbs 8:29; Jeremiah 5:22). The oceans can only hint at the power of God:

THE SEAS HAVE LIFTED UP, O LORD,

THE SEAS HAVE LIFTED UP THEIR VOICE;

THE SEAS HAVE LIFTED UP THEIR POUNDING WAVES.

MIGHTIER THAN THE THUNDER OF THE GREAT

WATERS, MIGHTIER THAN THE BREAKERS OF THE

SEA—THE LORD ON HIGH IS MIGHTY.

(PSALM 93:3-4)

17

MOUNTAINS

Only a few things in this world deserve to be called mountains. Towering at least 2,000 feet above sea level, mountains cover a fifth of earth's land area, while submarine ranges spread over most of the sea floor ◆ These natural elevations in the earth's crust generally form by folding, faulting or volcanic activity. At an elevation of 19,347 feet, Ecuador's Cotopaxi dwarfs all other active volcanoes. The highest peak in North America is Alaska's Mt. McKinley (20,320 feet), while at 29,028 feet, the highest mountain in the world remains Mt. Everest in the Himalayas ◆ As friction from subducting plates begins to build, some mountains crack wide open, spewing lava, steam, ash and poisonous gases. Before May 1980, Mt. Saint Helens rose to 9,677 feet above sea level. Her explosion blasted more than 1,000 feet off her peak and triggered a series of disasters: flash floods and mudslides, clouds of ash spreading all over the world, over 100 square miles of denuded forests. More than 150 miles of trout and salmon streams were destroyed, along with 26 lakes. Sixty-six persons and an estimated 2 million animals died in the blast ◆ Yet the Mt. Saint Helens disaster pales in comparison to others. A late-night eruption of Nevado del Ruiz in Colombia in 1985 sent a wave of mud across the town of Armero, killing 23,000 sleeping citizens. And a 1902 eruption of Mount Pelee on Martinique released a blast of hot gases that killed all but two of the town's 30,000 residents. Who can grasp the power of an angry mountain?

AND YET...

G od has merely to look at the earth, and it trembles; He touches the mountains, and they smoke (Psalm 104:32). Massive as mountains are, He moves them without their knowing it and overturns them in His anger (Job 9:5). By His infinite wisdom and power He created the world's peaks (Psalm 65:6) as a picture of His righteousness (Psalm 36:6). When we gaze at them we should think of Him, and along with the Psalmist declare to our Lord,

YOU ARE RESPLENDENT WITH LIGHT,

MORE MAJESTIC THAN MOUNTAINS

RICH WITH GAME.

(PSALM 76:4).

DESERTS

You want hot? Then visit a desert. In their most sizzling months, earth's deserts may average from 105 to 110 degrees Fahrenheit. Not scorching enough for you? Then plan a trip to the Sahara, which holds the record at a blistering 136 degrees. And don't worry about finding a place to enjoy the heat; the vast Sahara sprawls over 3.5 million square miles, an area roughly the size of the United States • How about dry? Chile's Atacama Desert holds the planetary record for aridity: not a single drop of rain has fallen there in more than 40 years. Many deserts rely on less than 10 inches of rain per year, with an evaporation rate 20 times the annual precipitation rate • Still, lack of moisture does have its benefits. Antarctica's dry polar deserts dip in temperature to an annual mean of about 1.5 degrees. In the Gobi desert of central Asia, inhabitants can expect as much as a six-month break from the heat; of course, they also have to contend with severe blizzards caused by ferocious winter winds • Speaking of winds, gale force storms have been known to throw millions of tons of sand hundreds of miles across the earth's deserts. Africa's Namib Desert has built dunes as high as 800 feet (only a little shorter than New York's Rockefeller Center, standing at 850 feet). While deserts cover 25 percent of the earth's surface, sand accumulates on less than 20 percent of their domain. For the real king of sand, consider Mars. With an atmospheric pressure of about one-hundredth that of Earth, our red neighbor boasts three million square miles of sand — an area greater than the Empty Quarter of Saudi Arabia, the largest sand sea on our planet.

AND YET...

W hen God wants water, He can produce it even in the desert. "They did not thirst when he led them through the deserts," marvels Isaiah. "He made water flow for them from the rock; he split the rock and water gushed out" (48: 21). Nor is God dismayed by the heat or sand, for when He wants arid Israel to bloom, "he will make her deserts like Eden, her wastelands like the garden of the LORD" (Isaiah 51:3). He spreads a table in the desert for His people (Psalm 78:19) and promises,

I WILL PUT IN THE DESERT THE CEDAR AND THE ACACIA, THE MYRTLE AND THE OLIVE. I WILL SET PINES IN THE WASTELAND, THE FIR AND THE CYPRESS TOGETHER, SO THAT PEOPLE MAY SEE AND KNOW, MAY CONSIDER AND UNDERSTAND, THAT THE HAND OF THE LORD HAS DONE THIS, THAT THE HOLY ONE OF ISRAEL HAS CREATED IT.

(ISAIAH 41:19-20)

VALLEYS

Lush. Green. Rich. Wide. When you think of fertile valleys, terms like these usually come to mind • A river or stream usually flows along valley floors, watering the rich soil and providing ideal growing conditions. The Willamette Valley in Oregon, a region more than 150 miles long and up to 30 miles wide, gets much of its water from the Willamette River and has earned a reputation for exports of fruit, dairy, and lumber. Just to the east lies an even more spectacular terrestrial depression: Hell's Canyon, the deepest gorge in North America, cut out of ancient lava flows on the Oregon/ Idaho border by the Snake River. In places it plunges 6,000 feet or more below the adjacent uplands • The world's deepest valley is found along a section of the Indus River in Kashmir. This valley drops about 23,000 feet from the top of its drainage divide to the bottom of the valley floor. Its steep slope erodes the riverbed at up to .4 inches each year • One of the largest valleys in the world is the Mississippi River Valley in the central United States, while the Great Rift Valley in Africa extends from Ethiopia to Mozambique. While most valleys received their v-shape from the rivers that formed and flow through them, others created by glacial action appear u-shaped. The latter tend to have steep sides and broad, flat floors. Glaciers formed Yosemite Valley, with its near-vertical walls. Some glacier-formed valleys, such as Sognafjorden in Norway, plunge below sea level and extend more than 70 miles inland • What awe these gorgeous valleys inspire in us!

AND YET...

No valley, no matter how fertile, produces abundance on its own. It is God who ensures "the valleys are mantled with grain; they shout for joy and sing" (Psalm 65:13). When He is angry, the Lord splits valleys apart "like wax before the fire, like water rushing down a slope" (Micah 1:4). On the day Jesus returns to rule the earth, God says He will raise up every valley (Isaiah 40:4) — but He will also create a new one:

ON THAT DAY HIS FEET WILL STAND ON THE MOUNT OF OLIVES, EAST OF JERUSALEM, AND THE MOUNT OF OLIVES WILL BE SPLIT IN TWO FROM EAST TO WEST, FORMING A GREAT VALLEY, WITH HALF OF THE MOUNTAIN MOVING NORTH AND HALF MOVING SOUTH.

(ZECHARIAH 14:4)

"The mark of a successful man is one who has spent an entire day on the bank of a river without feeling guilty about it," said one Chinese philosopher, and it's hard to argue with him. While rivers represent only one four-thousandth of the earth's total fresh water, they play an enormous role in the planet's health ✦ River floodplains, terraces and alluvial fans not only offer visual delight, they are essential to feeding millions around the world. They also

RIVERS

provide a source of shelter and sustenance for 50 percent of the earth's 1,200 endangered animal species. When rivers go unprotected, devastation results — witness the Cuyahoga River in northeastern Ohio, which literally caught fire when careless factories dumped large quantities of hydrocarbon waste into the water ✦ The Amazon River in South America is the world's largest by volume. It carries up to twenty-five percent of all the water running off the earth's surface and discharges about 6.35 million cubic feet of water into the Atlantic each second, turning the ocean from salty to brackish for 100 miles out to sea. It's not the world's longest river, though; that distinction belongs to the Nile, with a length of 4,132 miles. If you were to stretch the Nile across the United States, it would run almost from New York to Los Angeles ✦ Rivers range anywhere from narrow and long to short and roaring. The River Rhone, generally regarded as the swiftest river in the world, attains a velocity of 40 miles per hour over some parts of its course. Colorado's wild rivers and tributaries sport names such as Satan's Gut, Hell's Half Mile, Disaster Falls, the Big Drop, and Skull Rapids (where three rafters died in November 1970). Never underestimate rivers!

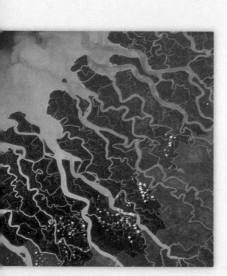

AND YET...

The Bible proclaims it is God who opens
up springs and streams, who dries up the
ever-flowing rivers (Psalm 74:15). God turned
the waters of the Nile into something like blood
(Exodus 7:20) and caused the Jordan at flood-
tide to pile up in a heap so that the ark of God
might cross over on dry land (Joshua 3:13). And
rivers remind us of our Lord's infinite love:

**HOW PRICELESS IS YOUR UNFAILING
LOVE! BOTH HIGH AND LOW AMONG
MEN FIND REFUGE IN
THE SHADOW OF
YOUR WINGS. THEY
FEAST ON THE ABUN-
DANCE OF YOUR
HOUSE; YOU GIVE
THEM DRINK FROM
YOUR RIVER OF
DELIGHTS.**

(PSALM 36:7-8)

EARTHQUAKES

When the solid earth rocks and rolls beneath our feet and the landscape suddenly disappears into black nothingness, fear grips the stoutest heart — and we know it can be but one thing: earthquake! ◆ About 50,000 earthquakes large enough to be noticed without instruments occur each year; about 100 of these can cause astonishing damage. Enormous quakes occur somewhere in the world about once each year. One of the biggest rocked Shaanxi Province in China in 1556, when an estimated 830,000 people died in the violent shaking. A 1964 quake in Alaska released at least twice as much energy as the one that flattened San Francisco in 1906. The Alaskan quake permanently tilted some 72,000 square miles of land, thrusting it as high as 80 feet at one end and sinking it 9 feet at the other ◆ Most quakes occur at the boundary of huge, slowly-moving plates which constantly bump into each other over the surface of the earth. More than half follow the "Ring of Fire" around the Pacific Rim, subjecting those who live near Japan, the Andes Mountains and the San Andreas fault to regular tremors. At least one town in California knows far more about quakes than it would like to. Parkfield, which sits atop the San Andreas fault, has averaged one quake every 22 years since 1857. If a massive quake were to hit the city of Tokyo, economists estimate that Japan's Gross National Product would plummet by almost a quarter, sending the world into a severe recession. Such staggering power prompted historian Will Durant to exclaim, "Civilization exists by geological consent, subject to change without notice."

AND YET...

T he only consent that matters is God's. It is He who "shakes the earth from its place" (Job 9:6). It is He who summons earthquakes to announce both His arrival (Exodus 19:18) and His departure (Matthew 27:51, 54). In the future He will use earthquakes in judgment (Ezekiel 38:19; Revelation 6:12; 8:5; 11:13; 16:18). The earth trembles at God's majestic presence (Nahum 1:5). But the best is yet to come:

THIS IS WHAT THE LORD ALMIGHTY SAYS: "IN A LITTLE WHILE I WILL ONCE MORE SHAKE THE HEAVENS AND THE EARTH, THE SEA AND THE DRY LAND. I WILL SHAKE ALL NATIONS, AND THE DESIRED OF ALL NATIONS WILL COME."

(HAGGAI 2:6-7)

They called it the "Dust Bowl." When rainfall fell an average of ten to twenty percent and the temperature rose about 1.5 degrees, a section of the Great Plains suffered a severe drought lasting a decade (1931-1940). Heavy spring winds, combined with overgrazing and poor land management, carried off the region's exposed topsoil, creating "black blizzards" that blocked out the sun and piled dirt in huge drifts. Sometimes these clouds of dust swept all the way to the East Coast, forcing thousands of families to leave their homes at the height of the Great Depression ◆ Droughts occur when, over a long time, evaporation and "transpiration"— the movement of water in the soil through plants into the air — exceed precipitation. In almost every corner of the globe, drought is the most serious threat to agriculture and is the world's most common natural cause of famine ◆ Drought-induced famines in northern China caused from 9 to 13 million deaths in 1876-1879, sparking

DROUGHT

cannibalism and prompting many parents to sell off their children. Another drought in India and Bengal (1769-1770) killed up to a third of the total population. In the Soviet Union, a two-year drought beginning in 1921 affected up to 24 million people and caused an estimated 1.5 to 5 million deaths. Even today, a prolonged drought that began in the late 1970s in eastern and southern Africa covers 2.6 million square miles and endangers 24 million people in up to 22 countries ◆ Even when drought doesn't kill, it ravages. During the 1950s, a seven-year water shortage devastated the economy of the Great Plains. By the time it was over, 244 of 254 Texas counties were declared federal disaster areas. A five-year drought in the 1960s dried up 25 percent of New York City's reservoirs, while a 1988 drought cost the U.S. $40 billion, surpassing the economic damaged inflicted by Hurricane Andrew, the Mississippi River floods of 1993, and the San Francisco earthquake of 1989. With destructive power like this, droughts have terrorized humankind for centuries.

AND YET...

The Bible says it is God who sometimes holds back the waters to cause drought (Job 12:15) as punishment for sin (Jeremiah 14:1-7). "Because of you the heavens have withheld their dew and the earth its crops," God told ancient Israel. "I called for a drought on the fields and the mountains" (Haggai 1:11). But for those who put their trust in God, not even drought has the power to terrify:

BLESSED IS THE MAN WHO TRUSTS IN THE LORD, WHOSE CONFIDENCE IS IN HIM. HE WILL BE LIKE A TREE PLANTED BY THE WATER THAT SENDS OUT ITS ROOTS BY THE STREAM. IT DOES NOT FEAR WHEN HEAT COMES; ITS LEAVES ARE ALWAYS GREEN. IT HAS NO WORRIES IN A YEAR OF DROUGHT AND NEVER FAILS TO BEAR FRUIT.

(JEREMIAH 17:7-8)

H ow do you describe a cloud? Do you opt for scientific terms—nimbus, cirrus, stratus, cumulus— or do you lean toward more poetic options like "wispy," "curly," "feather-like," "stringy," or even "puffy"?   •   Clouds form when moist air rises. Low pressure at higher altitudes allows masses of air to expand, cooling until their temperature drops below the dew point, when the air becomes supersaturated. Excess water purely of ice crystals. At the other extreme, clouds may descend all the way to earth; these clouds (cumulonimbus) we call fog   •   Clouds serve a significant role in balancing our world's climate. Were it not for their day job of reflecting harmful amounts of sunlight back into space, the earth would soon become inhospitably hot. Were it not for their efforts after dark, the earth would too quickly cool as waves of heat escaped into space. Beautiful clouds may fill us with delight as we see them floating regally overhead, but we're only beginning to discover how they operate.

CLOUDS

vapor then condenses onto microscopic dust or smoke particles, quickly forming non-precipitating water droplets about 0.0004 inch in diameter; most clouds have a density of about a thousand of these droplets per cubic inch. The vast majority of clouds consist of a combination of water droplets and ice crystals, ice predominating at higher altitudes   •   Clouds vary widely in shape, size, location and life span. Most clouds drift high above our heads at altitudes from 6,000 to 45,000 feet, although they may soar to 60,000 feet. These high clouds (cirrus) consist

AND YET...

G od knows exactly how clouds do their work, for He gave them their jobs (Job 36:27-29). He counts them all (Job 38:37) and summons them (Genesis 9:14) "to punish men, or to water his earth and show his love" (Job 37:13). God makes black clouds and deep darkness his canopy (Deuteronomy 4:11) and "makes the clouds his chariot and rides on the wings of the wind" (Psalm 104:3). No wonder Moses cried out,

THERE IS NO ONE LIKE THE GOD OF JESHURUN, WHO RIDES ON THE HEAVENS TO HELP YOU AND ON THE CLOUDS IN HIS MAJESTY.

(DEUTERONOMY 33:26)

RAIN

Before a single drop of rain falls from the sky to refresh the earth, it spends about ten days in flight. It rarely grows larger than about .15 inch in diameter, and when it shrinks to less than .02 inches by the time it reaches earth, we call it drizzle • Most rain descends at an average rate of three to thirty drops per cubic foot—but not all, as Unionville, Maryland, discovered on July 4, 1956. On that day the town recorded 1.23 inches of rain in one minute. Twelve inches of rain fell in one hour at Holt, Missouri, on June 22, 1907; 73.6 inches deluged Cilaos on Reunion Island on March 16, 1952; and 366 inches soaked Cherrapunji, India, in one sopping month, during the same year the region set the annual rainfall record of 1,042 inches (August 1860-July 1861) • Want to grow a single serving of lettuce? It'll cost you six gallons of rainwater. How about a glass of milk? You'll need almost 49 gallons of the wet stuff to produce just one eight-ounce glass of the white stuff (the amount of water consumed by the cow + the amount needed to produce her food + the water to process it all). Like a serving of steak with that? Only 2,600 gallons more—not much of a problem if you live near Mt. Waialeale, Hawaii, which averages 450 inches of rain per year, but a big problem if home is Iquique, Chile, where rain hasn't fallen in 14 years • While we need rain to survive, we don't want too much of it. Since 1900, floods have killed more than 10,000 people in the United States alone. In 1976, the Big Thompson Canyon Flood in Colorado swept away 139 people, 95 percent of whom unwisely tried to outrun the deluge. The flood of 1993 along the Mississippi River covered an area some 500 miles long and 200 miles wide, severely damaging nearly 50,000 homes and 12,000 square miles of farmland. For the entire month of June, 1972, Rapid City, South Dakota, endured a series of heavy rains and floods that took the lives of 237 residents and inflicted $100 million in property damage. If only we could control the rain!

AND YET...

God does control the rain, every last drop of it (Job 28:26). It is God who cuts a channel for the watery torrents (Job 38:25). The Lord promised Israel He would open the storehouse of His bounty to send rain on the land in season (Deuteronomy 28:12) — but also that He would withhold rain when His people rebelled (Isaiah 5:6). So the prophet Jeremiah declares

DO ANY OF THE WORTHLESS IDOLS OF THE NATIONS BRING RAIN? DO THE SKIES THEMSELVES SEND DOWN SHOWERS? NO, IT IS YOU, O LORD OUR GOD. THEREFORE OUR HOPE IS IN YOU, FOR YOU ARE THE ONE WHO DOES ALL THIS.

(JEREMIAH 14:22)

STORMS

The weapons of humankind may cause us to tremble, but what can compare with the awesome might of storms? It wasn't Japanese naval power, but nature, that nearly torpedoed the World War II career of Admiral William "Bull" Halsey. The American admiral regularly outfought and outmaneuvered his Imperial enemies, but two typhoons sank several of his ships late in the war, sending nearly 1,000 sailors to a watery grave. Many observers wanted Halsey punished for failing to take his fleet out of harm's way • From ordinary rain showers to tornadoes, from snowstorms and thunderstorms to tropical cyclones, violent atmospheric disturbances send us running for cover. A storm in August 1994 sent two 80,000-pound tractor-trailers flying 600 miles away. In 1997 near Jarrell, Texas, tornadoes ripped the asphalt straight off the road. A ferocious storm in Des Arc, Arkansas, killed two parents but spared their baby, who suffered only minor bruises after being carried aloft 300 yards into a barren field. And during a 1915 storm in the small farming community of Great Bend, gusts of wind hurled five horses a quarter mile from their barn, while the same winds slaughtered a thousand sheep • Sometimes, one storm begets another. Thunderstorms, for example, often spawn multiple tornadoes. In a 24-hour period between April 3 and 4, 1974, one thunderstorm gave birth to 148 tornadoes in 13 states — with 15 twisters on the ground simultaneously. No one knows for sure how strong tornadoes may grow, but their winds have been clocked at up to 318 mph (the wind gauge broke at that point). Storms are nothing to ignore, as Admiral Halsey found out too late.

AND YET...

S cripture tells us that "lightning and hail, snow and clouds, stormy winds" all do God's bidding (Psalm 148:8). In fact, God's "way is in the whirlwind and the storm, and clouds are the dust of his feet" (Nahum 1:3). The Lord spoke to Job out of a storm (Job 38:1; 40:6); He used a storm to put the prophet Jonah back on track (Jonah 1:4); and just before the Exodus He whipped up "the worst storm in all the land of Egypt since it had become a nation" (Exodus 9:24). Yet He is our "shelter from the storm" (Isaiah 25:4), as the disciples discovered in Matthew 8:24–26.

THEN THEY CRIED OUT TO THE LORD IN THEIR TROUBLE, AND HE BROUGHT THEM OUT OF THEIR DISTRESS. HE STILLED THE STORM TO A WHISPER; THE WAVES OF THE SEA WERE HUSHED. THEY WERE GLAD WHEN IT GREW CALM, AND HE GUIDED THEM TO THEIR DESIRED HAVEN.

R oy Sullivan of Virginia personally disproved that lightning never strikes twice. Before he died in 1983, the retired forest ranger survived no fewer than seven lightning strikes. Actually, most people struck by lightning do survive (about four survivors for every fatality), but they don't remember the incident; lightning usually disrupts normal memory formation. Some people have even

LIGHTNING

regained their sight after getting hit by lightning. For those whose shocking experience provided less positive results, however, a support group exists: The Lightning Strike and Electric Shock Victims International   •   Lightning hits the earth 100 times each second, with 8.6 million strikes per day and over 3 billion each year. Each strike occurs in the blink of an eye — actually, considerably less than that. When positive and negative charges crash into each other, they create the explosive flash we recognize as lightning. Their meeting lasts all of one ten thousandth of a second   •   Cool, no? Ah, but it's really terribly hot. A single bolt of lightning can heat the surrounding air from 15,000 to 50,000 degrees Fahrenheit — up to five times the surface temperature of the sun. And what of the lightning itself? An average bolt packs a wallop of several hundred million volts, with peak currents of up to 20,000 amperes   •   Lightning can appear in many shapes and sizes — even colors. Ball lightning takes a grapefruit-size shape, soaring and spinning and glowing in bright shades of red, orange or yellow. This rare form of electricity has been reported to boil tubs of water, burn barns and melt

wires. It usually leaves behind a trademark sizzling sound and sulfuric odor   •   During active thunderstorms, wise humans avoid high elevations or spots in which they become the tallest feature (as on a golf fairway), since lightning usually strikes upraised targets. The National Center for Health says lightning kills about 80 Americans each year, while the Los Angeles Times claims lightning may injure up to 1,500 each year. A word to the wise: if you're ever in Florida — the top state for fatal lightning strikes — don't go golfing in the rain. More than a wayward golf ball may hit you.

AND YET...

God directs the course of lightning and asks us, "Do you send the lightning bolts on their way? Do they report to you, "Here we are"? (Job 38:35). Bolts of lightning proceed out of the brightness of His presence (Psalm 18:12) to light up the world (Psalm 97:4).

LISTEN! LISTEN TO THE ROAR OF HIS VOICE, TO THE RUMBLING THAT COMES FROM HIS MOUTH. HE UNLEASHES HIS LIGHTNING BENEATH THE WHOLE HEAVEN AND SENDS IT TO THE ENDS OF THE EARTH. AFTER THAT COMES THE SOUND OF HIS ROAR; HE THUNDERS WITH HIS MAJESTIC VOICE. WHEN HIS VOICE RESOUNDS, HE HOLDS NOTHING BACK. GOD'S VOICE THUNDERS IN MARVELOUS WAYS; HE DOES GREAT THINGS BEYOND OUR UNDERSTANDING.

(JOB 37:2-5)

Wind may be just a puff of air, but what a puff it may be • In ancient times, Sirocco winds in the Sahara Desert wiped out an entire Persian army. Greeks claimed that the northerly winds of southern France could hurl men from their chariots. In the eastern Rockies and southern California, a Foehn wind (also known as a Chinook or a Santa Ana) can raise the air temperature by forty-nine degrees in two minutes, melt several yards of snow in hours, ripen corn, and unglue

WIND

furniture. Near Sydney, Australia, winds known as "brickfielders" may raise coastal temperatures to 120 degrees • If you've ever endured the winds of a tornado, you'll never forget the ordeal. About 800 tornadoes are reported each year, causing a yearly average of 80 deaths worldwide and more than 1,500 injuries • But hurricanes create the mightiest winds of all. 1998's Hurricane Mitch caused an estimated 11,000 deaths in Central America, obliterated nearly 100 bridges in Honduras alone and destroyed 95 percent of that nation's crops. In 1900 a deadly hurricane surged across Galveston Island, Texas, killing between 6,000 and 12,000 residents. The Great Hurricane of 1780 near Martinique left an

estimated 22,000 people dead. And storm tides caused by cyclones (what hurricanes are called in the southern hemisphere) off the coast of Bangladesh killed hundreds of thousands of persons in 1970 • Why do the swirling walls of a hurricane cause so much damage? Because they store an enormous amount of energy. In one day, a typical hurricane generates the energy equivalent to that released by 400 twenty-megaton hydrogen bombs. If such energy could be harnessed and converted to electricity, it would fuel the electrical needs of the United States for about six months.

AND YET...

God stores even the strongest winds safely in His heavenly closet. It is God who "brings out the wind from his storehouses" (Psalm 135:7). Our God called for wind to make the global waters recede in Noah's day (Genesis 8:1) and He commanded another wind to part the Red Sea in Moses' day (Exodus 14:21). When a violent wind frightened the apostles, the Lord Jesus calmed it with a word (Mark 4:39). Wind may seem unimaginably powerful, but it is nothing but an obedient servant of the Lord:

HE MAKES THE CLOUDS HIS CHARIOT AND
RIDES ON THE WINGS OF THE WIND.
HE MAKES WINDS HIS MESSENGERS,
FLAMES OF FIRE HIS SERVANTS.

(PSALM 104:3, 4)

FIRE

I n 1827 an English chemist named John Walker harnessed a force that has fascinated, thrilled, terrified and amazed humankind from the very beginning. Walker applied phosphorous sulfate to a wooden stick and invented . . . the friction match. And so was fire contained ✦ Or, maybe not ✦ Lightning sparks some 7,500 forest fires in the United States every year, about twenty fires a day. In 1997, a massive forest fire in southeast Asia sent a thick haze over six countries — Malaysia, Singapore, Brunei, Indonesia, the Philippines and Thailand— affecting 70 million people and prompting the closure of countless factories, offices and schools. In 1871, one wildfire in Wisconsin killed 1,152 people and blackened a record 1.8 million acres ✦ So much for "containing" fire ✦ Home fires can consume a house in minutes. Experts advise anyone trapped in such a conflagration to crawl along the floor, since temperatures in a burning home can vary from 100 degrees at floor level to 600 degrees at eye level. If the rapidly-spreading flames don't kill,

superheated air, smoke or poisonous gases released by intense heat often do. Every year more than 4,000 Americans die and another 25,000 are injured by fiery infernos ✦ Yet were it not for fire, the world's ecosystems would be left in grave jeopardy. Many forests and grasslands depend upon regular fires to consume decaying matter and weed out diseased and harmful organisms, thus making room for reforestation, enhanced wildlife habitats, and reducing the chances for catastrophic fires. Once massive blazes begin, no power yet harnessed by man can contain them — John Walker's invention notwithstanding.

AND YET...

The Bible describes God Himself as "a consuming fire" (Deuteronomy 4:24; Hebrews 12:29). When the Lord gave the Law to His people, "Mount Sinai was covered with smoke, because the LORD descended on it in fire" (Exodus 19:18). God spoke to David through fire (1 Chronicles 21:26), endorsed the ministry of Elijah by sending fire from heaven (1 Kings 18:24, 38), and opened the eyes of Elisha's servant so that he could see the heavenly army protecting his master, with "the hills full of horses and chariots of fire all around Elisha" (2 Kings 6:17). Truly,

OUR GOD COMES AND WILL NOT BE SILENT; A FIRE DEVOURS BEFORE HIM, AND AROUND HIM A TEMPEST RAGES.

(PSALM 50:3)

ICE

Most substances contract when cooled. Not so water—and we should be grateful that's so. Since ice is less dense than its liquid counterpart, it floats. If it sank, the oceans of the world would freeze solid and make life as we know it impossible. A world covered by ice and snow would reflect most of the sunlight that struck it, and the average temperature of our planet would plunge to minus 128 degrees Fahrenheit ⬩ About three quarters of the earth's fresh water is stored in glaciers that cover about 11 percent of the world's land area. The Antarctic, perpetually covered by an ice sheet more than a mile deep, contains ninety-one percent of the world's glacier ice—thereby making it by far the highest continent on earth (1.3 miles, compared to less than .6 miles for all others). If all this ice were to melt, sea levels would rise about 300 feet ⬩ It's easy to forget about ice, but it affects our lives in important ways. For example, major shipping routes could be shortened by as much as 30 percent if we could safely navigate through the Arctic Ocean—but icebergs prevent it. Since ice and snow poorly reflect radar, even an iceberg 22 feet high can't be detected if it's riding waves higher than four feet. Visual tracking is still the only effective way of keeping tabs on dangerous icebergs, so to this day ship captains are forced to proceed at slow speed in fog. Many modern nations have tried to find efficient ways to destroy icebergs, with little success. Attempts at bombing, torpedoing, shelling and ramming these floating mountains of ice have all met with spectacular failure.

ND YET...

G od creates these icy behemoths with a little puff from his nostrils (Job 37:10). At His command the water becomes hard as stone and thick frost covers the earth (Job 38:29). Snow and ice are nothing more than servants obedient to every whisper of His word, eager to freeze or flow at His pleasure:

HE SPREADS THE SNOW LIKE WOOL AND SCATTERS THE FROST LIKE ASHES. . . WHO CAN WITHSTAND HIS ICY BLAST? HE SENDS HIS WORD AND MELTS THEM; HE STIRS UP HIS BREEZES, AND THE WATERS FLOW.

(PSALM 147:16-18)

43

HAIL

Never underestimate the power of a little drip. Especially when it falls in the form of hail ◆ These ice droplets begin their short lives in the upper reaches of thunderstorms, growing as they ascend through successive layers of freezing updrafts. The colder the cloud and the faster the updraft, the bigger the stone. Most of these icy chunks never get bigger than a dime, and many melt before ever touching the ground. But some expand to the size of golf balls, baseballs, even grapefruit. And when the updrafts can no longer keep them aloft, these frozen stones hurtle toward the earth at speeds approaching 90 miles per hour. ◆ Because of the way they form, hailstones develop stratified interiors and multiple layers, resembling a frozen onion more than a sphere of solid ice. Still, they don't disintegrate easily; golf-ball-size hail striking the earth has been known to bounce anywhere from one to two feet high. Most hailstorms last for about fifteen minutes, occur in the middle to late afternoon and at the beginning of a thunderstorm, and never when the ground temperature is below freezing ◆ Residents living in Hail Alley—South Dakota, Nebraska, Kansas, Oklahoma, western Texas, eastern Colorado, and eastern New Mexico—know well the sound of ice pellets smacking rooftops.

Sometimes hail announces the approach of tornadoes; at other times it arrives all on its own. But in either case it can strip trees of their leaves and limbs, crack or shatter auto windshields, devastate crops, damage buildings, and in the case of large chunks, injure exposed animals or people. Because hail can wreak such havoc, in 1939 the federal government began an all-risk crop insurance program to protect interested farmers from financial ruin in case of crop failure caused by natural disasters, including hail. Sure, they're only little drops of water—but you'd be a fool to underestimate them.

AND YET...

Hailstones represent merely another item in God's heavenly arsenal. "He hurls down his hail like pebbles," declares Psalm 147:17. Isaiah says God uses hail to "cause men to hear his majestic voice" and to "make them see his arm" (30:30). God asked Job if he had "seen the storehouses of the hail, which I reserve for times of trouble, for days of war and battle?" (Job 38:22, 23). The Lord used hail to free the Israelites from Egyptian bondage (Exodus 9:19-25), to defeat the Amorites in Joshua's time (Joshua 10:11), and will use enormous hailstones in future judgment (Revelation 16:21). Yet those who trust in Him have nothing to fear:

MY PEOPLE WILL LIVE IN PEACEFUL DWELLING PLACES, IN SECURE HOMES, IN UNDISTURBED PLACES OF REST. THOUGH HAIL FLATTENS THE FOREST AND THE CITY IS LEVELED COMPLETELY, HOW BLESSED YOU WILL BE, SOWING YOUR SEED BY EVERY STREAM, AND LETTING YOUR CATTLE AND DONKEYS RANGE FREE.

(ISAIAH 32:18-20)

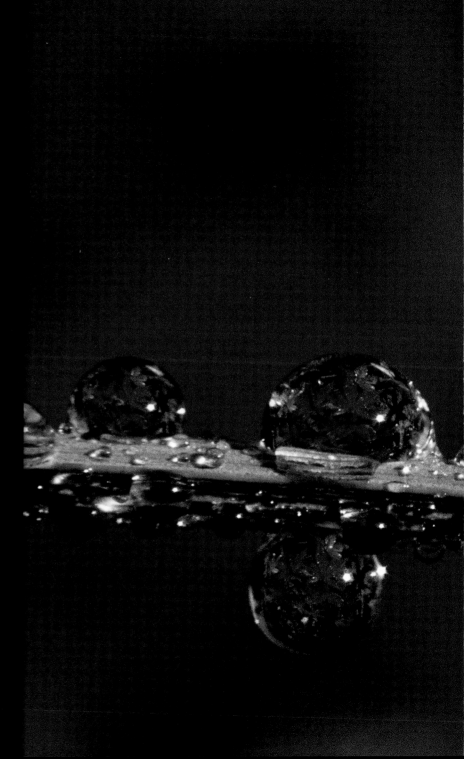

*S*weet *day, so cool, so calm, so bright, The bridal of the earth and sky, The dew shall weep thy fall to-night; For thou must die* ◆ So wrote George Herbert almost four centuries ago, poetically marrying the dew to the night. Dew, however, boasts more than a mere poetic connection to the night. It forms at night through condensation of water vapor when exposed surfaces—whether

◊ DEW

blades of grass, leaves, or garden hoses—lose heat through radiation to the sky. At a given temperature, air can hold only a certain amount of vapor, so as it cools, it bestows its moisture upon exposed surfaces, the watery deposit we call "dew." The temperature at which dew begins to form is called "the dew point." If the dew point dips below freezing, frost appears ◆ Dew can form downward from the atmosphere or upward from the ground. Total annual dew precipitation ranges from about .5 inches in cold climates to about 3 inches in semihumid, warm climates. In Israel and parts

of Australia, sufficient dew can be trapped for use in irrigation. In arid regions, dew has little importance, except in coastal deserts such as the Namib in southwest Africa, where humid breezes from nearby oceans allow plentiful dewfall. We cannot control the dew, but wherever it appears, we marvel at the beauty these little droplets of water can lend to an otherwise unremarkable landscape.

AND YET...

God brings forth the dew through His infinite wisdom (Proverbs 3:20), calling himself its Father (Job 38:28). He compares His gift of dew to His gift of everlasting life (Psalm 133:3) and promises He will be like the welcome dew to His dearly loved people (Hosea 14:5). Although He can at times remain as quiet and still as the dew (Isaiah 18:4), nevertheless, He is always working to bless His people, as His Word reminds us:

MAY GOD GIVE YOU OF HEAVEN'S DEW AND OF EARTH'S RICHNESS—AN ABUNDANCE OF GRAIN AND NEW WINE.

(GENESIS 27:28)

SILVER

While it may represent second place in the field of sports, silver remains the frontrunner in many other arenas ❖ From ancient times silver has been used as a medium of economic exchange. In early history travelers depended on silver vessels to preserve their water, wine, milk and vinegar during long voyages. Without silver nitrate, the first photographic image would not have developed in 1813. Silver made possible the creation of the first telegraph in 1832. And were it not for this precious metal, physicians in 1884 would not have invented a vaccine that saved generations of children from a lifetime of blindness ❖ Silver continues to work with other metals to power our world. Silver contacts inside electric switches help to operate numerous household appliances. Silver also labors in computer keyboards, behind automobile dashboards, and inside the control panels of washing machines and microwave ovens. Because of its superior lubricity, corrosion resistance, and thermal conductivity, silver gets used in jet engines and high-performance bearings. Silver-based alloys make possible high-power radar tubes and various electronic devices, with a melting range from 290 degrees Fahrenheit to more than 1,800 degrees. As a catalyst in numerous chemical reactions, silver makes possible the production of formaldehyde and many widely used household products, such as wood finishes, automotive parts, thermal and electrical insulation materials and toys ❖ Silver's amazing strength, malleability and ductility make it a metal without peer. There's no mystery why humankind has always prized this shiny, costly substance!

AND YET...

God warned Israelite kings not to collect large amounts of silver, or they would be tempted to forget Him (Deuteronomy 17:17). He forbade His people from making silver idols (Exodus 20:23) and predicted that one day the world would throw its idols of silver to rodents and bats (Isaiah 2:20). All the silver in the world belongs to God (Haggai 2:8), even though thirty silver coins were used to betray His Son (Matthew 26:15). Silver may be costly, but it cannot compare with the counsel of God:

THE WORDS OF THE LORD ARE FLAWLESS, LIKE SILVER REFINED IN A FURNACE OF CLAY, PURIFIED SEVEN TIMES.

(PSALM 12:6)

G old! Throughout human history, this shiny, malleable yellow metal has been used as a symbol of power and a means of exchange. In the tomb of the Egyptian pharaoh Tutankhamen, explorers found a 2,448 pound gold coffin filled with hundreds of gold and gold-leafed objects. Even today, gold remains by far the most significant means of international payment. Governments and central banks hold about 60 percent of all the gold ever mined • Gold never corrodes, never crumbles, never tarnishes. It is unaffected by moisture, oxygen or ordinary acids, and is one of the world's most efficient conductors of electricity. An ounce of it can be beaten out to a sheet covering 300 square feet • Gold connectors make possible the miracle of computers. Compact discs are sealed with protective gold coatings to prevent corrosion. Gold ensures that parachutes will deploy, radios will broadcast, airbags will inflate, and ejection seats will eject. Were it not for the gold-coated visors worn by Apollo astronauts on the moon — visors that reflected 98 percent of the sun's infrared radiation—the blazing light would have scorched the earth men's eyes • More than 5,000 years ago, physicians believed this precious metal possessed magical healing properties for "comforting sore limbs" (arthritis) and treating skin ulcers. Today, modern doctors still use gold in the treatment of rheumatoid arthritis and skin ulcers.

GOLD

AND YET...

Despite all its remarkable characteristics and indisputable economic power, gold pales in comparison to God's Living Word, which is "more precious than gold, than much pure gold" (Psalm 19:9-10). Jesus insisted the temple was far more precious than the gold that covered it (Matthew 23:17). Even "imperishable" gold will perish (Revelation 18:16), unlike the priceless blood of Christ (1 Peter 1:18, 19). Because ill-gotten gold corrodes spiritually (James 5:3), we are counseled to develop our faith, which is worth more than gold (1 Peter 1:7). Last, God promises we can look forward to the day when we will settle down in a city made

OF PURE GOLD, AS PURE AS GLASS . . . THE GREAT STREET OF THE CITY WAS OF PURE GOLD, LIKE TRANSPARENT GLASS . . . NOTHING IMPURE WILL EVER ENTER IT, NOR WILL ANYONE WHO DOES WHAT IS SHAMEFUL OR DECEITFUL, BUT ONLY THOSE WHOSE NAMES ARE WRITTEN IN THE LAMB'S BOOK OF LIFE.
(REVELATION 21:18, 21, 27).

PRECIOUS STONES

Y ou may like wearing a diamond or ruby or emerald— but would you eat one? ✦ Up to the 18th Century, gemstones played a curious role in popular medicine. Pope Clement VII, who died in 1534, is reported to have pulverized and consumed 40,000 ducats worth of precious stones for medicinal purposes (a ducat was a gold coin) ✦ Gems were also thought to convey special powers. Diamonds supposedly gave the wearer strength in battle and protected against ghosts and magic. Sapphires were to deflect poverty and betrayal, prevent eye diseases and cure snake bites. Emeralds were thought to break if a spouse proved unfaithful, and when placed under the tongue, they supposedly gave the gift of prophecy ✦ Of the approximately 2000 natural minerals thus far identified by science, fewer than 100 are regarded as gemstones, and only sixteen have become important commercially. A few organic materials are also considered precious stones, including pearl, red coral, amber, and ivory ✦ For millennia gemstones have been prized in jewelry and ornamentation. The green emerald was known in ancient Egypt as long ago as 1650 B.C., and jet (a dense variety of lignite formed by the submersion of driftwood in the mud of the seafloor) has been used since Roman times (and since it's a form of coal, it also burns). Whether it's due to their color, texture, or ability to refract light, precious stones continue to bedazzle human eyes.

AND YET...

God declares that the wisdom He wants to give us is of greater worth than rubies, topaz, coral, jasper or jewels (Job 28:17-19). The gemstones we consider so rare and prized, He intends to use as construction materials for the walls and gates and streets of His heavenly city (Isaiah 54:12; Revelation 21:11-21). Most of all, He wants us to outshine any gemstone:

THE LORD THEIR GOD WILL SAVE THEM ON THAT DAY AS THE FLOCK OF HIS PEOPLE. THEY WILL SPARKLE IN HIS LAND LIKE JEWELS IN A CROWN. HOW ATTRACTIVE AND BEAUTIFUL THEY WILL BE!

(ZECHARIAH 9:16, 17)

SEA MONSTERS

In the days of wooden sailing ships, sailors attributed missing vessels to attacks by sea monsters. Maps of the period dutifully noted unfriendly waters by the phrase, "Here there be sea serpents" ◆ While modern science has never spotted such terrifying beasts, it has studied some fearsome real-life sea monsters. Consider the sperm whale, a blunt-snouted mammal with an enormous head, a blocky profile and an underslung jaw with a row of large, conical teeth. The male can grow to a length of 62 feet and can dive to depths of 1,150 feet (it has been found tangled in cables at depths of 3,720 feet). It was an albino sperm whale that served as the villain in Herman Melville's *Moby Dick*—and history really does record rare attacks on humans. Sperm whales normally travel in herds of 15-20 and feed on cephalopods, including the giant squid ◆ Science knows of the giant squid only through the decayed carcasses that periodically surface; no human has ever seen one alive. Some recovered bodies have measured more than 65 feet long. Like its smaller kin, the giant squid has ten arms, including two long tentacles with broadened ends and four rows of suckers (some almost a foot in diameter) equipped with toothed, horny hooks. They use their tentacles to seize their prey and transfer it to their shorter arms, which feed it to the animal's huge, parrot-like beak. Giant squid have the largest eyes on earth, a necessary quality for life lived perpetually at depths of 985 – 1,970 feet below the surface ◆ For a creature less exotic but perhaps even more frightful, consider the great white shark. This sleek carnivore can grow up to 40 feet long and usually feeds on seals and sea turtles. It swims in tropical and temperate oceans worldwide and uses hearing, smell, sight, taste, touch and electrical perception to locate food, which it tears to pieces with rows of large, serrated, arrowhead-shaped teeth. A few years ago several great whites attacked and sank a dory off of Cape Breton, Nova Scotia; these great sharks often swallow objects half their size. Still, they have a ways to go to catch up with their extinct cousin, the Carcharodon megalodon. That shark grew up to 990 feet in length. Talk about a monster!

AND YET...

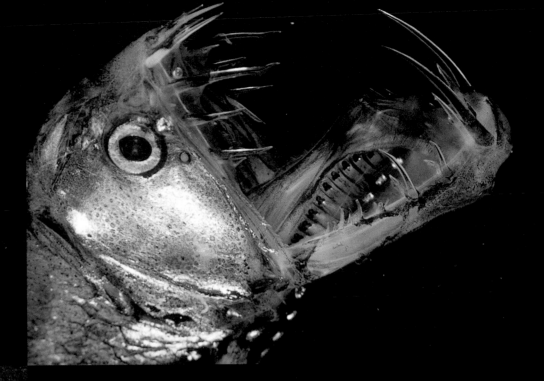

God created all the great creatures of the sea (Genesis 1:21) and is pleased to see them "frolic" there (Psalm 104:24-26). Even these awesome beasts are commanded to praise their Creator (Psalm 148:7) and it takes no effort at all for God to break "the heads of the monster in the waters" and to give his carcass "as food to the creatures of the desert" (Psalm 74:13, 14). Yet if foolish humans were to try such a feat, God promises,

YOU WILL REMEMBER THE STRUGGLE AND NEVER DO IT AGAIN! ANY HOPE OF SUBDUING HIM IS FALSE; THE MERE SIGHT OF HIM IS OVERPOWERING. NO ONE IS FIERCE ENOUGH TO ROUSE HIM. WHO THEN IS ABLE TO STAND AGAINST ME?

(JOB 41:8-10)

E ver wondered how the lion earned the title, King of the Jungle? Maybe he got it by virtue of impressive presence, his thick mane flowing from head to shoulders. Or perhaps he earned it by the way he carries himself, roaming the land in regal unconcern. Or, just maybe, he won it by possessing more ferocious abilities than other species, yet choosing for the most part to use none of them   ◆

LIONS

Although the lion possesses all the right tools — ferocious, wide jaws; powerful, hooked claws — for maintaining order within his kingdom, he seldom rouses himself, for he knows his harem will cover for him. The male lion leads a lethargic royal life, sleeping on average 21 hours a day   ◆ A dominant lion doesn't hunt every day; he leaves that to his harem. When the mood does strike him, a lion cautiously stalks his prey for two or three hours in the early evening, then uses his enormous body mass and momentum to run his victim into the ground, killing it with a fatal bite to the throat. Before the hunt, the lion issues a roar, which can be heard up to five miles away. If he's successful — which happens only a quarter of the time — he roars again to boast of his accomplishment. Members of the pride then come forward to take part in the feasting,

starting with the adult males, who sometimes devour as much as 90 pounds of meat in one setting. Why so much? Because they may go for a week or more before their next fill. Lionesses feed second, and cubs must fend for themselves, gorging on whatever remains   ◆   Oh, one last thing: the King of the Jungle really isn't, since he doesn't live in a jungle at all. The lion spends his lazy days in rich savannah grasslands. Another cat, the even larger tiger, prowls the jungle. So maybe we'd be better off calling the lion the King of Beasts?

AND YET...

Wile it may appear to us that the lion reigns high above all other beasts, he is weak and hungry in the eyes of the Lord (Psalm 34:10). God commands the lions to bow down, to shut their mouths and be still (Daniel 6:22). Although even the wise fear the lion, mighty among beasts (Proverbs 30:29-31), the Bible tells us that God created this magnificent cat to symbolize His own grace and beauty. The day approaches when we will see the King of kings and Lord of lords, striding among the hosts of heaven with regal dignity and pride. In that hour, every knee shall bow to Him and every tongue will confess His right to rule, and we shall all proclaim,

SEE, THE LION OF THE TRIBE OF JUDAH, THE ROOT OF DAVID, HAS TRIUMPHED.

(REVELATION 5:5)

EAGLES

Who can spot an eagle soaring in the heavens and not pause to marvel? The 59 species of eagles identified by science range throughout the world, each one specially adapted to its particular domain. Africa's harpy eagle and the Philippine eagle — among the largest species known — weigh more than 20 pounds each, with a wingspan of eight feet. Their fist-sized, razor-sharp talons are capable of killing and carting off prey as large as deer and monkeys. Eagles subsist primarily on live prey and try to surprise and kill their targets on the ground, often decapitating them ✦ Eagles mate for life and use the same nest every year, building it in high, remote places where they take six to eight weeks to rear a small clutch of eggs. Young eagles reach adult plumage by the third or fourth year of life ✦ While the eagle reigns supreme in the sky, it also has been known to take to the water. Eagles have been observed latching onto fish and surfing to shore. Some have been seen swimming — using their wings in an overhand movement, much like the backstroke ✦ And what a marvel are the eagle's piercing eyes! An eagle boasts five times the sensory cells of the human retina, enabling it to see objects twice as far away as anything our eyes can resolve. If eagles could read, they could absorb a newspaper from a mile away. Where humans see just three basic colors, eagles see five, enabling them to pick out even the most well-camouflaged of prey. It's even reported that some species can track an animal the size of a rabbit from up to two miles away.

AND YET...

While we wonder at the flight of the eagle, awesome and majestic to earthbound eyes, God guides every soaring movement of his flight (Proverbs 30:18-19). At His command, God instructs the eagle to climb to the uppermost regions of the sky and calls upon him to build his nest amongst the stars (Job 39:27; Obadiah 1:4). At the end of history, God will call upon the eagle to proclaim woe to an unrepentant planet (Revelation 8:13). Through the majesty of the eagle, God gives fresh hope to a creation far more beloved and infinitely nearer to His own heart:

BUT THOSE WHO HOPE IN THE LORD WILL RENEW THEIR STRENGTH. THEY WILL SOAR ON WINGS LIKE EAGLES; THEY WILL RUN AND NOT GROW WEARY, THEY WILL WALK AND NOT BE FAINT.

(ISAIAH 40:31)

T hough the name "snake" often conjures up images of evil, one cannot deny the impressive physical features of this infamous species. For a creature born without hands, paws, claws or legs, the snake is not the least bit handicapped. From head to tail— whether he measures five inches or thirty-one feet—he is fully capable of getting along   •   By contracting muscles on alternating sides of his body and by compressing his ribs, a snake is able to slither past potential obstacles, whether on land or sea.

SNAKES

One stumbling block he cannot surmount is the temperature; as a cold-blooded animal, he cannot survive in frozen conditions. To keep from wandering into inhospitable climates, snakes rely on heat-sensitive pit organs. Found on each side of the head

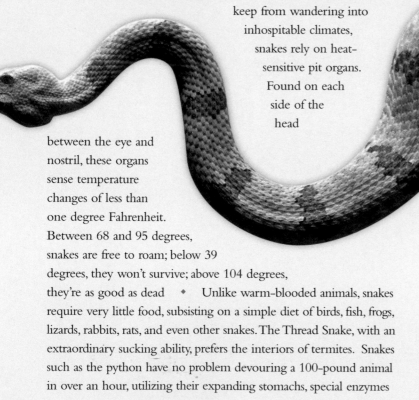

between the eye and nostril, these organs sense temperature changes of less than one degree Fahrenheit. Between 68 and 95 degrees, snakes are free to roam; below 39 degrees, they won't survive; above 104 degrees, they're as good as dead   •   Unlike warm-blooded animals, snakes require very little food, subsisting on a simple diet of birds, fish, frogs, lizards, rabbits, rats, and even other snakes. The Thread Snake, with an extraordinary sucking ability, prefers the interiors of termites. Snakes such as the python have no problem devouring a 100-pound animal in over an hour, utilizing their expanding stomachs, special enzymes

and retractable windpipes to do the job. When the weather is right, snakes bask in the sun to assist the digestive process.   •   Snakes also possess extremely well developed defenses. Some snakes use rattles to deter enemies; some imitate rattler behavior by drumming their tails between dry leaves; some play dead by coiling into a ball; some crush their victims with powerful constrictor muscles; and some simply bite. The African "spitting" cobra can squirt venom into the eyes of an enemy six to eight feet away, causing a painful burning sensation that can result in blindness. And a variety of the inland taipan of central Australia carries enough venom in a single bite to kill nearly 250,000 mice   •   Beware the serpent!

AND YET...

God commands even the bite of the serpent (Amos 9:3b) and has used the snake's deadly venom to discipline His people (Numbers 21:4-9). The God-designed movement of snakes over rocks amazed one biblical writer (Proverbs 30:18-19), and some Maltese islanders gasped when God protected the apostle Paul from a viper's bite (Acts 28:3, 4). But we will all stand amazed on the day when God changes the serpent's very nature:

THE INFANT WILL PLAY NEAR THE HOLE OF THE COBRA, AND THE YOUNG CHILD PUT HIS HAND INTO THE VIPER'S NEST. THEY WILL NEITHER HARM NOR DESTROY ON ALL MY HOLY MOUNTAIN, FOR THE EARTH WILL BE FULL OF THE KNOWLEDGE OF THE LORD AS THE WATERS COVER THE SEA.

(ISAIAH 11:8-9)

To call the locust a mere grasshopper is to badly misunderstand ◆ Locusts travel in huge swarms—up to 130 million per square mile. Imagine a locust onslaught stretching from Saskatchewan, Canada, all the way to Texas. One such insect army in 1889 covered 2,000 square miles near the Red Sea and weighed an estimated 42,850 million tons. Such enormous swarms of locusts have been known to block out all sunlight ◆ When not in flight, locusts depend on long hind legs to jump from one green meal to the next. One attack in 1870 by Rocky Mountain locusts lasted ten years and resulted in the destruction of millions of dollars worth of crops in the Mississippi Valley ◆ Even after they die, locusts continue to wreak havoc. Millions of decaying insect corpses have derailed locomotives and caused fatal highway accidents. In South Africa, mounds of dead locusts three to four feet high sprawled for 100 miles along the coastline, their stench traveling up to 150 miles inland ◆ Only extremely cold countries avoid catastrophic locust plagues. Those living everywhere else can expect at some point to witness swarms of locusts eating everything in sight, from bark, clothes, curtains, wool off sheep, and even one another. Locusts truly are an army to be reckoned with.

LOCUSTS

AND YET...

God called history's largest locust swarm "my great army" and sent it to do His will (Joel 2:25). Locusts without number follow His every order (2 Chronicles 7:13), advancing in ranks even though they have no king among them (Proverbs 30:27). The Lord is their King; when He speaks, the locusts swarm (Psalm 105:34). And when He speaks again, they march into the sea:

"I WILL DRIVE THE NORTHERN ARMY FAR FROM YOU, PUSHING IT INTO A PARCHED AND BARREN LAND, WITH ITS FRONT COLUMNS GOING INTO THE EASTERN SEA AND THOSE IN THE REAR INTO THE WESTERN SEA. AND ITS STENCH WILL GO UP; ITS SMELL WILL RISE." SURELY HE HAS DONE GREAT THINGS.

(JOEL 2:20)

TREES

B irds call them home. Squirrels abuse them as storage units. And we all know what dogs do to them. But there's more to a tree than what meets the eye • Every living creature— whether above the earth, on the earth, below the earth or in the sea—depends on these gnarled treasures. Through the process of photosynthesis, trees inhale carbon dioxide and exhale oxygen. Plant 30 trees each year and you offset the greenhouse gases from both your car and house; plant an acre and they'll release enough oxygen for eighteen individuals each day. At the same time, they will devour as much carbon dioxide as that produced by a vehicle driven 26,000 miles. By strategically planting trees around your house, you can cut your air conditioning bill in half • Tree leaves catch tiny particles of soot and dust that other- wise would damage human lungs. Tree roots maintain the soil by gathering minerals and water while securing the ground around them. Without these roots, erosion chokes streams and leads to serious flooding, while sedi- ment swirling in muddy creeks kills fish eggs and other wildlife • Trees are extremely resilient, surviving even in extreme weather. Even severe branch or limb breaks do not usually threaten a tree's life. It's easy to see why many cul- tures have long associated trees with life. The explorer Jacques Cartier reportedly was able to cure his scurvy-ridden crew by making tea from the vitamin C-laden bark of an Eastern white cedar. Even today we tap

trees to extract the active ingredients used in combating anything from asthma to coughs. The bark and needles of the yew tree yield an agent used to make taxol, an anti-cancer medicine. Trees mean so much to our quality of life that the humorist Ogden Nash, taking his cue from the famous poem by Alfred Joyce Kilmer, wrote,

"I think that I shall never see
A billboard lovely as a tree
Indeed, unless the billboards fall
I'll never see a tree at all."

AND YET...

E ven trees know that God is the real star, for as David said, "the trees of the forest will sing, they will sing for joy before the LORD" (1 Chronicles 16:33). The trees will burst into song on the day the Lord redeems His people (Isaiah 44:23) and will clap their hands in great joy (Isaiah 55:12). For all eternity we will look at a tree and remember the loving kindness of our God, for in the middle of our heavenly home there will stand

THE TREE OF LIFE, BEARING TWELVE CROPS OF FRUIT, YIELDING ITS FRUIT EVERY MONTH. AND THE LEAVES OF THE TREE ARE FOR THE HEALING OF THE NATIONS. . . BLESSED ARE THOSE WHO WASH THEIR ROBES, THAT THEY MAY HAVE THE RIGHT TO THE TREE OF LIFE.

(REVELATION 22:2, 14)

F lowers," wrote Ralph Waldo Emerson, "are a proud assertion that a ray of beauty outvalues all the utilities of the world."

♦ Recent studies prove flowers generate long-term, positive mood changes and can make people instantly happy. Feng Shui enthusiasts claim chrysanthemums bring laughter and happiness to one's home ♦ Humankind has for ages turned to flowers to express love and affection—and love doesn't come cheap. A tulip

FLOWERS

sensation in the 16th Century prompted bulbs to trade for up to 400 English pounds, roughly four million dollars in today's economy. But you'd better know what you're buying, since different flowers send varying messages. An acacia flower means "friendship;" a deep red rose means "bashful;" tulips mean "fame;" and a long stem yellow rose implies "decrease of love, jealousy." The carnation family has its own subtle differences: pink ("I'll never forget you"); striped ("Sorry I can't be with you"); and yellow ("Disdain") ♦ Not only do flowers promote emotional health, some improve physical health. Modern research suggests that substances found in mistletoe slow tumor growth. Practitioners of folk medicine believe they can cure patients of chilblains by beating them with holly until they bleed. Still, don't assume all flowers contain miracle substances. The Sacred Datura, with its attractive white petals, tinged with violet, exudes a fragrance like no other. But don't eat it! Its toxic seeds cause hallucinations, increased heart rate and distorted vision. Also keep your mouth away from the Monkshood, a deep, blue-purple flower. Ingesting it can cause muscle paralysis, gastrointestinal pains and even death. Renowned artist Georgia O'Keefe probably had nicer flowers in mind when she said, "When you take a flower in your hand and really look at it, it's your world for the moment."

AND YET...

While God loves the beauty of the flowers He created (Luke 12:27), He uses them most often to remind us how fleeting our days really are (Job 14:2; Psalm 103:15; James 1:10-11; 1 Peter 1:24). "All men are like grass, and all their glory is like the flowers of the field," says Isaiah. "The grass withers and the flowers fall, because the breath of the LORD blows on them" (40:6,7). Because that's true, our Lord invites us to put our faith in Him and refuse to worry about what life might bring.

SEE HOW THE LILIES OF THE FIELD GROW. THEY DO NOT LABOR OR SPIN, YET I TELL YOU THAT NOT EVEN SOLOMON IN ALL HIS SPLENDOR WAS DRESSED LIKE ONE OF THESE. IF THAT IS HOW GOD CLOTHES THE GRASS OF THE FIELD, WHICH IS HERE TODAY AND TOMORROW IS THROWN INTO THE FIRE, WILL HE NOT MUCH MORE CLOTHE YOU, O YOU OF LITTLE FAITH?

(MATTHEW 6:28-30)

GRASS

Aside from its rich color and pleasing appearance, grass offers countless life-enriching benefits. Every year, an average-sized lawn produces enough oxygen for a family of four. Grass also serves as a natural filter, purging the air of carbon dioxide, dust, dirt, and other pollutants, while reducing soil erosion and cooling the air. Perhaps the most commercially valuable grasses are found among the flowering plant order known as Poaceae: millet, corn (maize), wheat, and rice • From corn, we receive food for our tables, feed for our livestock and raw materials for our industries. Stalks are made into paper and wallboard; husks are used as filling material; cobs are used to make charcoal and industrial solvents • Ninety percent of all harvested wheat is used to make foodstuffs such as breads, pastas, cakes, crackers, cookies, pastries, and flours, while the remaining 10 percent is used to make industry by-products such as starch, paste, malt, dextrose, gluten, and alcohol • Rice farming serves a multitude of purposes even before the

harvest. Flooded rice fields function as holding ponds where harmful chemicals break down through natural ventilation and exposure to the sun. These purified waters return to rivers and streams, increasing the survival rates of fish stock. Migrating waterfowl like ducks, geese and shorebirds visit rice fields in search of fallen grain, weed seeds and aquatic insects, and fly away nourished, hefting extra weight for the winter, new, stronger feathers for the journey, and improved chances for successful breeding • What a comfort to know we have such a vital and abundant resource as grass!

AND YET...

None of these benefits come from grass itself, but from the Gardener, Our Heavenly Father. God makes even the desolate wasteland sprout with grass (Job 38:27), yet He also makes it wither with a single breath (Isaiah 40:7). God tells us not to fear powerful enemies, for He will wither them like grass (Isaiah 51:12), and one day in judgment He will burn up all of earth's green grass (Revelation 8:7). But until that day, the Bible reminds us that it is God alone who

MAKES GRASS GROW FOR THE CATTLE,

AND PLANTS FOR MAN TO CULTIVATE—

BRINGING FORTH FOOD FROM THE EARTH:

WINE THAT GLADDENS THE HEART OF MAN,

OIL TO MAKE HIS FACE SHINE, AND BREAD

THAT SUSTAINS HIS HEART.

(PSALM 104:14-15)

When we still ourselves for a moment and gaze in silent wonder at the awesome marvels of God's creation, who can resist a powerful urge to join the Psalmist in joyfully exclaiming, O LORD our Lord, how majestic is your name in all the earth! You have set your glory above the heavens ✦ Yet even as our hearts soar heavenward at the magnificence of God, we

GENTLE WHISPER

also come face to face with a troubling question, voiced long ago by the Psalmist:

> When I consider your heavens, the work of your fingers,
>   the moon and the stars, which you have set in place—
> What is man that you are mindful of him? (Psalm 8:1, 3, 4)

Our dilemma becomes even more pointed when we remember that all of creation—the stars, the sun, the moon, the earth, and all its wondrous creatures—are, in the words of the patriarch Job, "but the outer fringe" of God's works, providing us with only a "faint whisper" of Him. "Who then can understand the thunder of his power?" he asked, no doubt shaking his head and shrugging his shoulders (Job 26:14).

AND YET...

God so transcends our paltry ideas of majesty that when He wants to make himself known most clearly to His dearly loved children, He does it not through a thunder of almighty power, not in a shower of blinding light, not even by a torrent of irresistible force. He speaks most convincingly not through violent winds, powerful earthquakes or blazing fires. . . but in "a gentle whisper" (1 Kings 19:11-13). Let us remember that when we grow confused, anxious, or troubled. God invites us to personally experience His majesty by acting upon one of His great and calming promises:

FEAR NOT, FOR I HAVE REDEEMED YOU;
I HAVE SUMMONED YOU BY NAME; YOU ARE MINE.
WHEN YOU PASS THROUGH THE WATERS,
I WILL BE WITH YOU; AND WHEN YOU PASS
THROUGH THE RIVERS, THEY WILL NOT SWEEP OVER YOU. WHEN YOU WALK THROUGH THE FIRE,
YOU WILL NOT BE BURNED; THE FLAMES WILL NOT
SET YOU ABLAZE. FOR I AM THE LORD, YOUR GOD,
THE HOLY ONE OF ISRAEL, YOUR SAVIOR.

(ISAIAH 43:1-3)